AG 15 '12

COMANCHE
History and Culture

Helen Dwyer and D. L. Birchfield

Consultant Robert J. Conley
Sequoyah Distinguished Professor at Western Carolina University

Gareth Stevens
Publishing

Please visit our website, www.garethstevens.com. For a free color catalog of all our high-quality books, call toll free 1-800-542-2595 or fax 1-877-542-2596.

Library of Congress Cataloging-in-Publication Data

Dwyer, Helen.
Comanche history and culture / Helen Dwyer and D.L. Birchfield.
    p. cm. — (Native American library)
Includes index.
ISBN 978-1-4339-7414-4 (pbk.)
ISBN 978-1-4339-7415-1 (6-pack)
ISBN 978-1-4339-7413-7 (library binding)
1. Comanche Indians—History. 2. Comanche Indians—Social life and customs. I. Birchfield, D. L., 1948- II. Title.
E99.C85D89 2012
978.004'974572—dc23

                    2011049453

New edition published in 2013 by
Gareth Stevens Publishing
111 East 14th Street, Suite 349
New York, NY 10003

First edition published 2005 by Gareth Stevens Publishing

Produced by Discovery Books
Project editor: Helen Dwyer
Designer and page production: Sabine Beaupré
Photo researchers: Tom Humphrey and Helen Dwyer
Maps: Stefan Chabluk

Photo credits: AP/Wide World Photos: p. 37; Corbis: pp. 8 (Bettmann), 17 (bottom), 18, 23 (both), 33, 34 (top), 39 (Frank Trapper); Native Stock: pp. 19, 20, 21 (both), 24, 25 (both), 26, 27, 28, 29, 34 (bottom), 35, 36, 37; North Wind Picture Archives: pp. 13, 17 (top); Peter Newark's American Pictures: pp. 11, 12, 15, 16; Shutterstock: pp. 5 (Steve Bower), 7 (Stocksnapper), 30 (Steve Heap), 31 (Cucumber Images).

Printed in the United States of America

CPSIA compliance information: Batch #CS12GS: For further information contact Gareth Stevens, New York, New York at 1-800-542-2595.

CONTENTS

Words that appear in the glossary are printed in **boldface** type the first time they appear in the text.

INTRODUCTION

The Comanches are a people of Oklahoma. They are just one of the many groups of Native Americans who live today in North America. There are well over five hundred Native American tribes in the United States and more than six hundred in Canada. At least three million people in North America consider themselves to be Native Americans. But who are Native Americans, and how do the Comanches fit into the history of North America's native peoples?

THE FIRST IMMIGRANTS

Native Americans are people whose **ancestors** settled in North America thousands of years ago. These ancestors probably came from eastern parts of Asia. Their **migrations** probably occurred during cold periods called **ice ages**. At these times, sea levels were much lower than they are now. The area between northeastern Asia and Alaska was dry land, so it was possible to walk between the continents.

Scientists are not sure when these migrations took place, but it must have been more than twelve thousand years ago. Around that time, water levels rose and covered the land between Asia and the Americas.

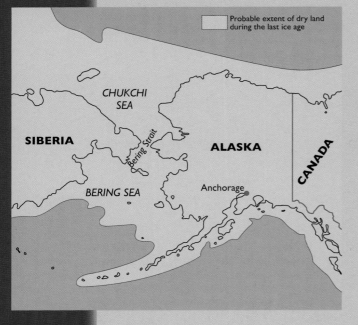

Probable extent of dry land during the last ice age

CHUKCHI SEA

SIBERIA

Bering Strait

ALASKA

CANADA

BERING SEA

Anchorage

Siberia (Asia) and Alaska (North America) are today separated by an area of ocean named the Bering Strait. During the last ice age, the green area on this map was at times dry land. The Asian ancestors of the Comanches walked from one continent to the other.

4

The Cliff Palace at Mesa Verde, Colorado, is the most spectacular example of Native American culture that survives today. It consists of more than 150 rooms and pits built around A.D. 1200 from sandstone blocks.

By around ten thousand years ago, the climate had warmed and was similar to conditions today. The first peoples in North America moved around the continent in small groups, hunting wild animals and collecting a wide variety of plant foods. Gradually these groups spread out and lost contact with each other. They developed separate **cultures** and adopted lifestyles that suited their **environments.**

SETTLING DOWN

Although many tribes continued to gather food and hunt or fish, some Native Americans began to live in settlements and grow crops. Their homes ranged from underground pit houses and huts of mud and thatch to dwellings in cliffs. By 3500 B.C., a plentiful supply of fish in the Pacific Ocean and in rivers had enabled people to settle in large coastal villages from Alaska to Washington State. In the deserts of Arizona more than two thousand years later, farmers constructed hundreds of miles of **irrigation** canals to carry water to their crops.

In the Ohio River valley between 700 B.C. and A.D. 500, people of the Adena and Hopewell cultures built clusters of large burial mounds, such as the Serpent Mound in Ohio, which survives today. In the Mississippi **floodplains**, the native peoples formed complex societies. They created mud and thatch temples on top of flat earth pyramids. Their largest town, Cahokia, in Illinois, contained more than one hundred mounds and may have been home to thirty thousand people.

CONTACT WITH EUROPEANS

Around A.D. 1500, European ships reached North America. The first explorers were the Spanish. Armed with guns and riding horses, they took over land and forced the Native Americans to work for them. The Spanish were followed by the British, Dutch, and French, who were looking for land to settle and for opportunities to trade.

When Native Americans met these Europeans, they came into contact with diseases, such as smallpox and measles, that they had never experienced before. At least one half of all Native Americans, and possibly many more than that, were unable to overcome these diseases and died.

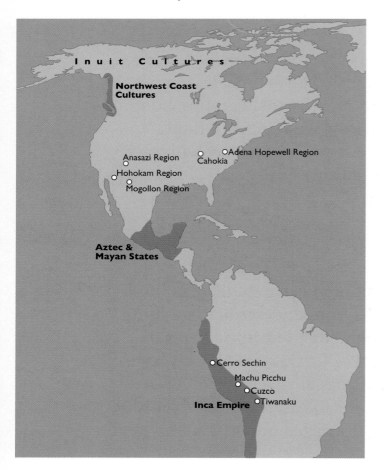

This map highlights some of the main early American cultures.

6

An illustration of a Comanche warrior on horseback in the 1800s.

Guns were also disastrous for Native Americans. At first, only the Europeans had guns, which enabled them to overcome native peoples in fights and battles. Eventually, Native American groups obtained guns and used them in conflicts with each other. Native American groups were also forced to take sides and fight in wars between the French and British.

Horses, too, had a big influence on Native American lifestyles, especially on the Great Plains. Some groups became horse breeders and traders. People were able to travel greater distances and began to hunt buffalo on horseback. Soon horses became central to Plains trade and social life.

During this time, the Comanches lived in the northern Rocky Mountains in what is today central Wyoming. They hunted large animals on foot, but after acquiring horses in the seventeenth century, they began to migrate to the southern Great Plains. This migration brought them into conflict with other native peoples and the Spanish across a wide area of present-day Colorado, Kansas, Oklahoma, Texas, and New Mexico. On the Great Plains, the Comanche lifestyle changed, and they hunted buffalo and made raids on other tribes on horseback.

At the end of the 1700s, people of European descent began to migrate over the Appalachian Mountains, looking for new land to farm and exploit. By the middle of the nineteenth century, they had reached the West Coast of North America. This expansion was disastrous for Native Americans.

In the 1840s, the United States took control of Texas and New Mexico. The Comanches fought to keep their land but were finally defeated in the 1870s.

RESERVATION LIFE

Many native peoples were pressured into moving onto **reservations** to the west. The biggest of these reservations later became the U.S. state of Oklahoma. Native Americans who tried to remain in their homelands were attacked and defeated. The Comanches were forced onto a reservation near the Wichita Mountains in Oklahoma.

New laws in the United States and Canada took away most of the control Native Americans had over their lives. They were expected to give up their cultures and adopt the ways and habits of white Americans. It became a crime to practice their traditional religions. Children were taken from their homes and placed in **boarding schools**, where they were forbidden to speak their native languages.

Despite this **persecution**, many Native Americans clung to their cultures through the first half of the twentieth century. The Society of American Indians was founded in 1911, and its campaign for U.S. citizenship for Native Americans was successful in 1924. Other Native American organizations were formed to promote traditional cultures and to campaign politically for Native American rights.

A group of Comanches wearing European-style clothes in a photo taken about 1890 in Washington, D.C.

THE ROAD TO SELF-GOVERNMENT

Despite these campaigns, Native Americans on reservations endured poverty and very low standards of living. Many of them moved away to work and live in cities, where they hoped life would be better. In most cases, they found life just as difficult. They not only faced **discrimination** and **prejudice** but also could not compete successfully for jobs against more established ethnic groups.

In the 1970s, the American Indian Movement (AIM) organized large protests that attracted attention worldwide. They highlighted the problems of unemployment, discrimination, and poverty that Native Americans experienced in North America.

The AIM protests led to changes in policy. Some new laws protected the civil rights of Native Americans, while other laws allowed tribal governments to be formed. Today tribal governments have a wide range of powers. They operate large businesses and run their own schools and health care.

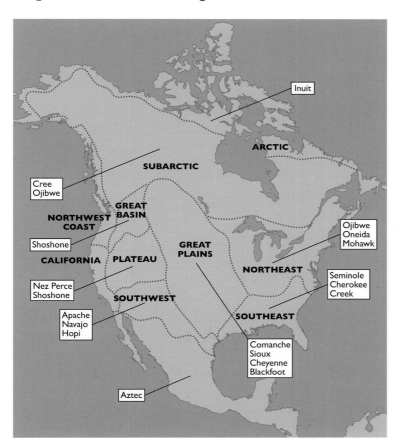

This map of North America highlights the main Native American cultural groups, along with the smaller groups, or tribes, featured in this series of books.

9

Chapter 1

LAND AND ORIGINS

COMANCHE COUNTRY

The Comanches are a North American native people with close to ten thousand tribal members. Many live near the Comanche **Nation** tribal headquarters in southwestern Oklahoma, while others live throughout North America.

Historically, Comanches were lords of the southern Great Plains, **dominating** a huge area from southern Kansas to central Texas and from eastern New Mexico to central Oklahoma. Their power was felt deep into Mexico, where ranchers feared their lightning-quick raids for cattle and horses.

HOW THE COMANCHES ARRIVED

Comanche origin stories tell of a time when great swirling winds from the four directions kicked up dust in a giant storm. The wind created a people with the power of storms and the strength of the earth from which they had been made.

The name *Comanche* might be of Spanish origin, from *camino ancho,*

As the red areas indicate, the Comanches migrated from Wyoming to the southern Great Plains. By the 1800s, they controlled much of present-day Kansas, Oklahoma, and Texas (as shown in violet).

Photographed in 1892, these two young Comanche girls are wearing traditional clothing.

meaning "the broad trail," referring to the Comanche raiding trails. The Comanche name for themselves is *Nerm* (sometimes *Neum, Nimenim,* or *Nununuh*), meaning "people of people" or "the people."

Comanche Words

The Comanche language is part of the Shoshonean language family. Most of the other tribes that speak Shoshonean languages (such as the Bannocks, Paiutes, Shoshones, and Utes) live in the northern Rocky Mountains or the Great Basin desert country of Nevada.

Comanche	Pronunciation	English
haa	hah	yes
ke	kay	no
kutu	koo-too	yesterday
tosa	tow-sah	white
hini	hee-nee	what?
hubi	hoo-bee	woman
toya	tow-yah	mountain
aho	ah-hoe	hello
kuhma	koo-mah	man

Chapter 2

THE HISTORIC MIGRATION

Comanches once lived in the northern Rocky Mountains in central Wyoming. They survived mostly by hunting deer and elk on foot, as they had for hundreds of years. Once they acquired horses in the late 1600s, however, the Comanches started moving to the southern Great Plains, and their lives changed quickly and dramatically. They became masters at hunting the huge southern buffalo herds.

Their migration south also changed the lives of many other people, both Indians and Europeans. By the early 1700s, the Spanish, who had entered the Southwest in the mid-1500s, began encountering Comanches in what is now southeastern Colorado.

TRYING TO STOP THE COMANCHE TIDE

The Comanche migration alarmed the Spanish because it threatened to disrupt Indian relations in New Mexico. The Spanish had made friends with the Plains Apaches, but now that tribe was in danger of being driven off the southern Great Plains by the arrival of the Comanches.

Artist George Catlin visited a Comanche village in Texas in the 1830s and made this painting. The women on the right are preparing a buffalo hide.

Artist Frederick Remington painted this Comanche man on horseback in the nineteenth century. A painter and sculptor, Remington captured aspects of Native American life, traveling all over the West.

The Plains Apaches asked for help from the Spanish, who built a fort in Plains Apache country to defend their friends. Nothing could stop the Comanches, however, who numbered in the thousands.

Sometime about 1724, many different bands of Plains Apaches came together to make one last desperate effort to hold back the Comanches. They fought a great battle, but the Comanches won, driving the Plains Apaches into the mountains of New Mexico. By the mid-1700s, the Comanches had taken control of the southern Great Plains all the way to central Texas.

An Abandoned Fort

In the early 1700s, the Spanish in New Mexico made great efforts to try to help their friends, the Plains Apaches, fight against the Comanche invasion. At great expense, the Spanish built a fort in present-day southeastern Colorado, beside the largest village of Plains Apaches, and stationed many soldiers there. (The fort, village, and Apache band all took the same name — El Quartelejo.) When an Apache got sick and died, however, the tribe moved its village many miles away because the Apaches always moved to a new place when someone died. The Spanish, unable to pick up their fort and move with them, had to give up trying to help their friends.

THE SPANISH COLONIAL ERA

During the mid-1700s, the Comanches made life miserable for the Spanish in New Mexico and Texas. There were so many Comanches — and so few Spanish soldiers — that Comanches raided the Spanish ranches at will, stealing horses by the thousands. Comanches soon became rich by trading the animals to other tribes farther north.

POLITICS ON THE PLAINS

This changed, however, in 1787 when the Comanches became military **allies** of the Spanish in New Mexico, and a great peace changed life for everyone in the region. The Comanches helped the Spanish fight the Apaches, the former allies of the Spanish who had been forced into raiding Spanish cattle herds after they had lost the buffalo plains to the Comanches. By 1790, the Spanish and Comanches were able to make almost all the Apaches stop raiding and settle near Spanish **missions**.

Iron Shirt

In 1787, Iron Shirt, a great military leader, was chief of the Comanches on the buffalo plains of eastern New Mexico. He convinced his people to make peace with the Spanish in New Mexico, which brought many advantages to the Comanches. They were then able to trade their buffalo meat and buffalo robes with the Spanish and the Pueblo Indians in New Mexico. The goods they received in exchange made life easier for the Comanches. These goods included Pueblo pottery and farm products, such as corn and beans, as well as Spanish trade goods, such as metal pots, guns, and ammunition.

That peace between the Spanish and the Comanches ended, however, during the chaos of the Mexican Revolution from 1810 to 1820. After Mexico won its independence from Spain in 1820, the Comanches considered their **alliance** over and went back to raiding whenever they wanted.

In 1848, the United States defeated Mexico in a war and acquired New Mexico as a territory. Texas had already gained its independence from Mexico in 1835 and had become a U.S. state in 1845. Comanches now faced a new and much stronger military power for control of the southern Great Plains — the United States.

Artist George Catlin was an eyewitness when Comanches greeted a U.S. cavalry troop on the Great Plains in 1835. Catlin sketched this drawing of their meeting.

TRYING TO CONTROL THE COMANCHES

The first attempt by the United States to establish its authority in the region was mostly **defensive**. The U.S. Army built a line of forts across the Texas frontier, hoping to restrict the Comanches' movements. The forts, however, did little to stop the Indians from doing as they pleased; the Comanches traveled throughout the region as they always had.

After the **Civil War** (1861–1865), the U.S. Army became more aggressive. Large armies defeated some Comanche bands, forcing them to move to a reservation under the **Treaty** of Medicine Lodge of 1867. However, the U.S. government did not provide food as it had promised in the treaty, so many of those Comanches rejoined their tribe on the Plains.

The Texas Rangers

In 1858, a special "Frontier Battalion" of soldiers called the Texas Rangers began making surprise attacks on Comanche villages outside the state of Texas, killing men, women, and children. The Texas Rangers taught the U.S. Army that Comanches could be attacked deep in their homeland, a lesson that the army was quick to learn and apply.

Carl von Iwonski painted *Terry's Texas Rangers* in 1845. The Texas Rangers were formed specifically to hunt down Indians, whether they lived in Texas or not.

These Indians require to be soundly whipped, and the ringleaders . . . hung, their ponies killed, and such destruction of their property as will make them very poor.

U.S. general William Sherman, 1868

THE WAR ON THE PLAINS

The end came swiftly for the Comanches. In 1874, in the Red River War, the U.S. Army launched a massive **campaign**, with many soldiers coming from forts in all directions. The soldiers had cannons and an early kind of machine gun, called a Gatling gun, that could fire four hundred shots a minute. The Comanches ran for their lives; the soldiers then burned their abandoned villages. At Palo Duro Canyon in the Texas Panhandle, the soldiers also shot and killed more than one thousand captured Comanche horses.

This photo shows an early type of army machine gun in the 1880s, known generally as a Gatling gun. This model was called a Maxim field gun.

As winter set in, the Comanches were left with nothing. Starving and freezing, they had little choice but to go to the forts and give themselves up. By the spring of 1875, virtually all the Comanches had surrendered. On the southern Great Plains, American hide hunters soon killed the last remaining buffalo on which the Comanches had depended. The old Comanche way of life ended, and the reservation era began.

Now a state park, Palo Duro Canyon in the Texas Panhandle, a place of great beauty, was a favorite site for Comanche villages.

On July 29, 1901, about thirty thousand people gathered to watch settlers trying to win their own section of Comanche lands in a lottery. The Comanches could only watch helplessly as most of their land was given to white settlers.

RESERVATION LIFE

Perhaps no other Indian people were less suited to reservation life than the Comanches. Long accustomed to riding free across the Plains, they suddenly found themselves on foot in present-day southwestern Oklahoma.

Their reservation, near the rocky and dry Wichita Mountains, was not well suited to farming, but the U.S. forced them to try to become farmers. Their children were taken from them and sent away to boarding schools.

LOSS OF THE LAND

U.S. treaties promised that Comanches would have their reservation forever, but by the late nineteenth century, land-hungry whites demanded the Comanche reservation land. In 1892, Congress forced the Comanches to accept individual ownership of small farms, called **allotments**, and sold the rest of the Comanche land to whites.

In 1907, Comanches were forced to become citizens of the new state of Oklahoma, and the U.S. government argued that the Comanche Nation no longer existed. Under the Indian Reorganization Act in 1934, however, the Comanches were allowed to form a joint business committee with the Kiowas and Kiowa-Apaches. That was the only form of government the Comanches had until their nation was allowed to organize a new government in 1963.

Throughout most of the twentieth century, the United States government and the state of Oklahoma tried to suppress Comanche culture, including religion, and to force Comanches to **assimilate** and become more like white people. Comanches would not have their own government again until late in the twentieth century. They still do not have all their land back.

Quanah Parker

Quanah Parker (1845–1911) was the son of a Comanche war chief and a white woman who had been captured by the Comanches. He too became a famous war chief and by 1890 was head of all the Comanche bands. On the reservation, he learned English quickly and helped the tribe raise money by leasing grazing land to whites. He was a judge on an Indian criminal court until the U.S. government removed him when it found out he had five Comanche wives. He managed his land and money so well that he became an **influential** leader of Indians on national issues.

Quanah Parker with two of his wives. The government refused to respect traditional Comanche marriages.

TRADITIONAL WAY OF LIFE

TRADITIONAL ECONOMY

The Comanche traditional **economy** was based on buffalo and horses. The great herds of buffalo on the southern Great Plains provided for almost all the Comanches' needs. Buffalo sinews, the tough, stringy tendons, made excellent bowstrings. Boiled down to make glue, even the buffalo hooves were put to use.

Buffalo meat provided more than fresh food. It could also be stored for winter food or trail food. This was done by cutting it into thin strips, salting it, and hanging it in the sun to remove most of the moisture. The dried meat was also pounded and mixed with nuts and berries to make a tasty, lightweight trail food known as pemmican.

A small buffalo herd near the Wichita Mountains in southwestern Oklahoma. Buffalo herds once roamed the southern Great Plains in huge numbers.

Chapter 3

This outdoor museum display allows visitors to see a tepee. At the right is a travois, a horse-drawn sled for moving heavy items.

While the hides supplied clothing and warm winter blankets, **tepees** made of buffalo hides gave the Comanches highly mobile homes. The long, slender pine poles that held up the tepee became the frame of a long sled, called a travois, when they moved. Carrying the buffalo hides that covered the tepees, the travois was dragged behind a horse.

Buffalo meat and hides also gave the Comanches valuable items for trade with other people, especially with the Spanish and the Pueblo Indians of New Mexico.

This museum display shows how Comanches prepared buffalo meat. The rack at the left is holding strips of meat for drying into buffalo jerky.

SUPERB HORSE TRADERS

Comanches became the greatest horse dealers in North American history. They had an endless supply of horses, stealing them by the thousands on raids in Texas and deep into Mexico. The Comanches traded the horses to tribes farther north on the Great Plains, becoming the main source of supply for a traffic that kept Indian tribes well mounted all the way to Canada.

From the mid-1700s to the mid-1800s, Comanches enjoyed a position of power and wealth that made them one of the most successful Native American groups in history. It made the change to reservation life especially difficult for a proud people who had achieved so much.

Comancheros

Comancheros were Mexicans and Americans who were engaged in a very dangerous line of work — conducting illegal trade with the Comanches. During the era of the Indian wars in the nineteenth century, the Comancheros operated out of New Mexico, driving wagons filled with trade goods far out onto the Plains to find the Comanches. The Comanches depended on the Comancheros for guns, ammunition, and other goods when they were at war and could not get those things from other sources. When Comanches were forced to accept reservation life, the Comanchero trade ended.

TRIBAL DIVISIONS

Comanches were never a unified political nation until after they were forced to accept life on the reservation. Over the past several hundred years, they have sometimes had as few as three tribal divisions and sometimes as many as twelve. Each one operated as an independent unit, with different territory on the buffalo plains. By the mid-nineteenth century, they had come to have six tribal divisions: Kwahada (Antelope), Nokoni (Wanderers), Penateka (Honey Eaters), Tenema (Downstream People), Kotsoteka (Buffalo Eaters), and Yamparika (Root Eaters).

Historically, the Comanches were remarkable for their success at avoiding the **temptations** of alcohol. Each warrior society was also capable of organized, coordinated military

Comanche war chief Mow-wi (Hand Shaker) once led the Kwahada (Antelope) band of Comanches.

An 1872 photo of Comanche leader Astlavi (also known as Milky Way or Bird Chief). He was a leader of the Penateka (Honey Eaters) band.

23

Comanches and Kiowas

Around 1790, the Comanches entered into a historic peace with the Kiowas that has never been broken. The two tribes traveled together, hunted together, and fought together against common enemies.

The two tribes could not have been more different, however. The Kiowas continually complained to the Comanches about being too hotheaded, too rash, and too ready to fly off the handle in an instant. The Comanches complained to the Kiowas that they would talk a problem to death rather than ever do anything about it. Together, they balanced one another's natural tendencies and maintained a remarkable partnership that controlled a huge expanse of land for a long time.

efforts, unlike many other Plains tribes, where each Indian was often his own boss. This difference made it possible for Comanche chiefs to plan military efforts almost like army generals.

These carved pieces of bone are dice crafted by Comanches. They were used in very popular gambling games.

TRADITIONAL GAMES

Comanches are a people who love to play games. One of their favorites is a dice game, made with dice carved from pieces of bone.

They also show great skill at their favorite game, the Indian hand game, which is popular among most Plains tribes. The hand game is a team sport. Seated in a row across from a rival team, team members rapidly pass a small item, often a bone, button, or bullet, from hand to hand. When the action stops, the rival team must guess which person actually holds the item. Comanches today can play the game for hours. In the old days, it provided entertainment on many cold days and nights in the winter tepees. Frequently, the game involved betting virtually everything valuable that team members owned.

A museum display of traditional Comanche clothing. The shirt is made of buckskin.

AN ARTISTIC PEOPLE

Comanche crafts are some of the most beautiful of the Plains Indians' art. Comanches excelled at making parfleches, finely crafted storage containers made of tanned elk hide. Colored

Comanche parfleches were used for storing and transporting food and other items. Many native groups produced beautifully designed parfleches.

A museum display of moccasins. Note the fine beadwork, carefully crafted by Comanche women.

with natural dyes and decorated with beadwork and porcupine quills, some are beautiful works of art.

Shirts, dresses, and moccasins made from deer and elk hides were also finely crafted and beautifully decorated. Comanches take pride in their appearance, and the women fashioned clothing that was both functional and attractive.

BELIEFS

Comanche culture is deeply religious. Traditional Comanches believe in an afterlife and revere the Great Spirit. They engage in periods of **fasting** and seek **visions** to help guide them in life. Traditional Comanches had great confidence in the power of **medicine men** to cure illness, interpret dreams, and guide the nation in times of crisis.

Where Did the Museum Get That?

Many of the historic Comanche craft items in museums and private collections were stolen from families during the period when Comanches were being forced to accept reservation life. During that era, many Americans believed that Indians had no rights. Soldiers stole items. Indian agents and missionaries stole items. Traditional clothing worn by Comanche children when they were sent to boarding schools was taken away from them and not returned. Many of those items ended up in museums. Today, Comanches and other Indians are demanding their things be returned to them.

Made from tiny beads, this medallion necklace is displayed at the Oklahoma Natural History Museum.

A buffalo skull painted for ceremonial use.

A MISLEADING MEDICINE MAN

In 1874, however, a young Comanche medicine man, Isatai, told people he had **supernatural** powers. He gained a large following, including war chief Quanah Parker. Isatai said that if the Comanches held a Sun Dance, they would be safe from the bullets of the American hide hunters who were killing all the buffalo.

In June 1874, the Comanches held the Sun Dance, which is a ceremony of dedication to the welfare of the tribe. After the ceremony, Isatai and Quanah Parker led a large force of Comanches in an attack on a small group of buffalo-hide hunters at Adobe Walls, Texas. When the buffalo-hide hunters killed several Comanches at great distances with their new high-powered buffalo guns, the natives withdrew, and Isatai lost his following. After these events, Comanche medicine men lost their influence in the tribe. Quanah Parker and most of the other Comanche leaders never believed in their powers again.

The Native American Church

Beginning in the 1880s, Quanah Parker became a strong supporter of using peyote, a drug that comes from the cactus plant, in Indian religious ceremonies that the Comanches learned from the Lipan Apaches. He traveled widely to Indian

A museum display of fans and rattles used in ceremonies of the Native American Church.

communities across North America, helping found what later came to be officially called the Native American Church. Many Comanches joined this church in the early 1900s. For most of the twentieth century, the federal government and the various states persecuted members of the Native American Church with harsh drug laws. Today, members of the church are no longer subject to those laws.

Comanche Origins

Many Comanche and other native legends tell of how things came to be the way they are today. Here are two of these Comanche stories.

THE BUFFALO ESCAPE

Originally, all buffalo were kept in captivity by a mighty creature called Humpback. They lived in a corral with high stone walls. The only way out was through the back door of Humpback's house, which was joined to the corral.

The cunning Coyote wanted to release the buffalo. He noticed that Humpback's young son did not have a pet, so he changed himself into a bird called a killdeer and waited by a spring until the boy passed by. The killdeer pretended his wing was damaged, and the boy picked him up and took him home. But when Humpback saw the killdeer, he was suspicious and refused to have the bird in his house.

The killdeer is a species of plover, and like many plovers, it pretends to be injured to lure predators away from its young. This is the behavior that Coyote copied in the story.

Coyote decided to try again, but this time he changed into a puppy. Once again, the boy found him and took him home. Once again, Humpback was angry, and he threatened to kill the puppy. The boy cried until Humpback agreed to let the puppy stay, as long as it remained in the corral.

That night, when Humpback and his son were asleep, the puppy quietly opened the back door of the house. He began chasing the buffalo, barking and biting their heels. The terrified animals stampeded through the house and escaped. From that time, the buffalo spread out across North America.

SPRING FLOWERS IN TEXAS

A very long time ago, the Comanche people in Texas were in grave trouble. No rain had fallen for a long time, so the ground was dry, nothing grew, and the people and animals were starving. The leaders asked the Great Spirit what they must do, and the Great Spirit replied that the people must **sacrifice** something of great value.

A young orphan girl began to think about how she could help. The only thing she loved very much was a doll with a blue face and blue feathers in its hair. Her grandmother had made the doll, and the girl slept with it every night. Sadly, she realized what she must do. In the middle of the night, she went outside and stood by the fire. The girl asked the Great Spirit to send rain and then threw the doll onto the fire. When the fire went out, the girl gathered up the ashes and threw them into the wind.

In the morning, rain began to fall and a few days later, plants with blue flowers grew all over the hills. Since then, every spring, masses of blue flowers called bluebonnets have bloomed in Texas to remind people of the little girl's sacrifice.

The bluebonnets in this story are a kind of lupin. They are now the official state flower of Texas.

Chapter 4

COMANCHES TODAY

THE COMANCHE NATION

For nearly a hundred years after the Medicine Lodge Treaty of 1867, the Comanches were formally joined with the Kiowa and Kiowa-Apache tribes. During much of the twentieth century, they conducted their affairs with a joint business committee made up of representatives of all three tribes.

In 1963, however, the Comanches organized the Comanche Nation of Oklahoma. Their tribal headquarters is located north of the small city of Lawton, near the Wichita Mountains of southwestern Oklahoma. Today around half of the nation's fifteen thousand members live in this region. The tribe holds elections every three years. Johnny Wauqua was elected Tribal Chairman in 2011.

In recent centuries, Comanches have been a people on the move, migrating from the northern Rocky Mountains to the southern Great Plains. The Comanche Nation's headquarters is now near Lawton, Oklahoma.

LaDonna Harris

An influential leader, Comanche writer LaDonna Harris (born in 1931) publishes articles about how Comanches and other tribes can start businesses and create jobs for their people. She grew up among her people and spoke only the Comanche language until she started school. In 1965, she founded an organization called Oklahomans for Indian Opportunity that helps Indian people have better lives. Then in 1970, she joined with other activists to form Americans for Indian Opportunity, which helps enrich the lives of all native groups and has links with other **indigenous** peoples around the world.

LaDonna Harris meets with an Indian woman in 1973. Harris has been one of the most active national leaders for Indian people, opposing discrimination in housing and other areas.

BUSINESS SUCCESSES
In 1995, under the leadership of Wallace Coffey Jr. as tribal chairman, the Comanches successfully issued their own license plates for tribal members' cars, despite the protests of the state of Oklahoma. In the 1990s, the Comanches joined with the Kiowas and Kiowa-Apaches in developing a water recreation park. The nation has also built four **casinos**, which provide the tribe with most of its income.

In modern times, Chief Wallace Coffey Jr. continued the great tradition of leadership of his people displayed by Comanche chiefs of past eras.

In 2002, the tribally controlled Comanche Nation College in Lawton was opened. The college offers higher education combined with Comanche customs and traditions and other Native American **philosophies.**

LIFESTYLES

Ever since the allotment of tribal land was completed in 1906, the Comanches have lived scattered throughout their former reservation, mixed in with the general rural population of southwestern Oklahoma. Many are farmers and ranchers or live in the small towns in the region. Many others are scattered throughout the continent, pursuing the same kinds of careers as other Americans. Most Comanche children now attend public schools in Oklahoma. Today, their activities and interests are very similar to those of other children in Oklahoma.

Medicine Bluff Creek in the Comanche homeland near the Wichita Mountains of southwestern Oklahoma.

A Culture Grows Stronger

Over the last few decades, Comanches have been experiencing a cultural **revival**. After a century of intense attempts by the U.S. government to make them give up their Indian ways and blend into the larger European American culture, Comanches are now being allowed to publicly embrace their traditions again. It is a huge change from one hundred years ago, when most Americans assumed that both the Comanche people and their culture would disappear forever.

In 1972, one of their old warrior societies, the Little Pony Society, was revived to honor returning Comanche Vietnam War veterans. In 1976, the Yamparika division of the Comanches revived their Black Knives Society. Once made up of some of the best warriors in the nation, those societies had been inactive for nearly a century.

Modern-day Comanche Warrior Society members in traditional dress gather for a tribal meeting in southwestern Oklahoma.

Other Comanche societies have become active again, including the Comanche Gourd Society and the Comanche War Dance Society. The War Dance Society was recently given permission by the Osage Nation to perform the Osage Heluska Society's Straight War Dance, an honor rarely given to another Indian nation.

Young Comanches demonstrate a competition powwow dance for visitors to Indian City, USA, a popular tourist attraction near Anadarko, Oklahoma.

Comanche Homecoming

An annual event, the Comanche Homecoming takes place in mid-July at Walters, a small town in southwestern Oklahoma. The powwow was started in 1952 to honor returning Comanche Korean War veterans and has been continued since then as the homecoming powwow. During Homecoming, Comanches camp together, renew old friendships, and visit with relatives.

LITERATURE AND THE ARTS

Comanches have been leaders in expressing modern-day Native American issues and concerns to non-Indians. Comanche writer Cornel Pewewardy is one of the most active Indian writers trying to get Americans to stop using Indians as **mascots** for sports teams. His articles on that issue have appeared in many publications. He has also had a distinguished career in education, becoming the youngest school principal on the Navajo Reservation. In 1991, the National Indian Education Association named him Indian Educator of the Year for his work with an Indian school in Minnesota. He is currently Associate Professor

of Native American Studies at Portland State University. A performing artist of traditional Comanche flute music, Pewewardy has recorded a number of compact discs, including *Spirit Journey* (1993) and *Dancing Buffalo* (1994).

Chief Illiniwek, the University of Illinois's mascot, was a student who danced in Indian clothing at sports events. The mascot's last appearance was in 2007.

Princess competitions are popular events in many tribes in Oklahoma, and this Comanche girl has just won the contest.

Paul Chaat Smith coauthored one of the most influential books about the American Indian Movement (AIM) of the late 1960s and early 1970s. His book, *Like a Hurricane*, describes how AIM members staged protests in the United States that brought worldwide attention to the poverty and hopelessness on many reservations. The **media** attention caused Congress to change many laws and to allow Indians more religious freedom and a chance to have better lives. In 2001, Paul Chaat Smith became Associate Curator of the Smithsonian's National Museum of the American Indian in Washington, D.C. He was a consultant for the TV series *We Shall Remain: A Native History of America*, which was shown in 2009.

Comanche poet Juanita Pahdopony has been an inspiration to young Comanche writers. She has helped conduct many workshops where young Indians learn how to get their poetry and other writing published. She teaches at the Comanche Nation tribal college in Lawton, Oklahoma.

Comanche Nation Buffalo Herd

Of all the recent changes in the Comanche Nation, perhaps none is more symbolic or more meaningful for the people than the beginning, in 2001, of a Comanche Nation buffalo herd. Buffalo meat contains a natural substance that fights **diabetes**, a disease from which many Indians suffer.

LOOKING TO THE FUTURE

While many Comanches are reestablishing their cultural roots, many are also active leaders in the business, professional, and political life of Oklahoma. Comanches work as doctors, lawyers, and managers; some are teachers, school administrators, and college professors. The Comanches have also produced great poets and scholars.

The most valuable resource of the Comanche Nation is its people. They have endured enormous hardships and have survived to enter the twenty-first century with renewed hope for the future.

Comanche actor Gil Birmingham at the premiere of *The Twilight Saga: New Moon* in 2009, in which he played Billy Black. A TV actor since the 1980s, Gil Birmingham starred in the miniseries *Into the West* in 1995.

TIMELINE

late 1600s	Comanches separate from the Shoshones and begin leaving central Wyoming for southern Great Plains.
1680	Comanches obtain horses after the Pueblo Rebellion.
early 1700s	Comanches and Utes form an alliance and attack the Apaches.
1720s	Spanish in New Mexico try helping friendly Plains Apaches hold back Comanches from driving Apaches off the Plains.
about 1724	Apaches lose big battle with Comanches, who take control of the southern Great Plains.
1740	Comanches obtain firearms from French traders.
1745	Comanches force Utes from the Plains.
mid-1700s	Comanche wars against the Spanish and several native tribes.
1787	Comanche leader Iron Shirt makes historic peace with the Spanish in New Mexico. Comanches begin trading with the Spanish and with Pueblo Indians.
late 1780s	Comanche warriors join Spanish soldiers and Navajo warriors in tracking down hostile Apaches and forcing them to live near Spanish missions, bringing a short era of peace to the region.
1790–1803	Comanches enter into historic peace with the Kiowa tribe; they fight wars against the Osage and Pawnee tribes.
1810–20	Long, bloody Mexican Revolution brings chaos to the Southwest; Indian peace breaks down.
1835	First Comanche treaty with United States; Texans fight Comanches as Texas ranchers move deeper into their homeland.
1840	Comanches and Kiowas enter into historic peace with the Cheyennes, become allies in wars with United States.

1848	United States gains New Mexico as a U.S. territory.
1858	Texas Rangers begin attacking Comanches outside of Texas.
1867	Treaty of Medicine Lodge establishes a joint Comanche, Kiowa, and Kiowa-Apache reservation.
1874–1875	U.S. Army defeats the Comanches in the Red River War.
about 1880	Last remaining buffalo are hunted to extinction, ending traditional Comanche way of life.
1892	Congress forces Comanches to accept individual allotments.
1907	Comanches forced to become citizens of Oklahoma.
1918	Native American Church officially founded.
1934	Comanches form a joint business committee with the Kiowas and Kiowa-Apaches.
1941–45	Comanches in U.S. Signal Corps use a signal code based on the Comanche language in World War II.
1963	Comanches establish Comanche Nation of Oklahoma.
1990s	Comanches open a bingo operation; join with Kiowas and Kiowa-Apaches to open a water recreation park.
1993	Comanche Language and Cultural Preservation Committee formed to preserve Comanche language and culture.
2002	Comanche Nation College is opened in Lawton, Oklahoma.
2003	First official Comanche Dictionary is published, compiled entirely by Comanches.
2007	Comanche National Museum and Cultural Center opens in Lawton, Oklahoma.
2011	Johnny Wauqua is elected Tribal Chairman of the Comanche Nation.

GLOSSARY

alliance: an agreement between two or more groups to work together.

allies: groups who agree to work together for a common goal.

allotment: forcing Indians to accept individual ownership of small farms, rather than all Indian land being owned by the tribe as a whole.

ancestors: people from whom an individual or group is descended.

assimilate: to be forced to adopt the culture — the language, lifestyle, and values — of another group.

boarding school: a place where children must live at the school.

campaign: large-scale army movements to attack.

casinos: buildings that have slot machines, card games, and other gambling games.

Civil War: 1861 to 1865 war between Northern and Southern states.

culture: arts, beliefs, and customs that make up a people's way of life.

defensive: guarding or protecting against attack.

diabetes: disease in which there is too much sugar in someone's blood.

discrimination: unjust treatment usually because of a person's race or sex.

dominating: having influence or control over something.

economy: how people make a living, how they feed themselves and provide for their other needs.

environment: objects and conditions all around that affect living things and communities.

fasting: refusing to eat anything for a time.

floodplain: the area of land beside a river or stream that is covered with water during a flood.

ice age: a period of time when the earth is very cold and lots of water in the oceans turns to ice.

indigenous: originating in a particular country or region.

influential: being able to affect what other people do or say.

irrigation: any system for watering the land to grow plants.

mascots: persons or animals adopted as good-luck symbols for teams.

media: television, newspapers, and other forms of communication.

medicine men: spiritual or religious leaders who are also healers.

migration: movement from one place to another.

mission: a church or other building where people of one religion try to teach people of another religion their beliefs.

nation: people who have their own customs, laws, and land separate from other nations or peoples.

persecution: treating someone or a certain group of people badly over a period of time.

philosophies: theories, attitudes, or beliefs that guide a person's or a group's behavior.

prejudice: dislike or injustice that is not based on reason or experience.

reservation: land set aside by the U.S. government for one or more specific Indian tribes to live on.

revival: an act of giving new strength; a renewal.

sacrifice: to offer something to the gods as an act of worship; often involves killing an animal or a person.

supernatural: beyond the natural world.

temptation: strong appeal.

tepee: a portable conical tent made of skins, cloth, or canvas on a frame of poles.

treaty: an agreement among two or more nations.

visions: things seen or experienced that are not from this world but the supernatural one; they resemble dreams, but the person is awake.

MORE RESOURCES

WEBSITES:

http://digital.library.okstate.edu/encyclopedia/entries/C/CO033.htm
A history of the Comanches from the Oklahoma Historical Society.

http://php.indiana.edu/~tkavanag/asoule.html
Includes photos of a Comanche village in the 1870s.

http://www.amitmay.com/pahdopony.htm
Web pages about the poet and artist Juanita Pahdopony, including photos of some of her artworks with her own comments and a poem.

http://www.bigorrin.org/comanche_kids.htm
Online Comanche Indian Fact Sheet for Kids in question-and-answer form with useful links.

http://www.comanchelanguage.org/
The website of the Comanche Language and Cultural Preservation Committee includes pages on the Comanche language, alphabet, and traditional culture.

http://www.comanchenation.com/
The official website of the Comanche Nation of Oklahoma.

http://www.native-languages.org/comanche.htm
This website has links to online Comanche language resources.

http://www.native-languages.org/comanche_animals.htm
Photos of animals with their Comanche names and a pronunciation guide.

http://www.texasindians.com/comanche.htm
Click down this page to find out more about Comanches and their ways. Site includes several maps.

DVD:

500 Nations. Simply Home Entertainment, 2007.

BOOKS:

Cunningham, Kevin, and Peter Benoit. *The Comanche (True Books: American History).* Children's Press, 2011.

De Capua, Sarah. *The Comanche (First Americans).* Benchmark Books, 2006.

Egan, Tracie. *Cynthia Ann Parker: Comanche Captive (Primary Sources of Famous People in American History).* Rosen Publishing Group, 2003.

Englar, Mary. *The Comanche: Nomads of the Southern Plains (American Indian Nations).* Capstone Press, 2006.

Englar, Mary. *Comanche Warriors (Warriors of History).* Capstone Press, 2008.

Gibson, Karen Bush. *Native American History for Kids: With 21 Activities.* Chicago Review Press, 2010.

Golden, Nancy. *Life with the Comanches: The Kidnapping of Cynthia Ann Parker (Great Moments in American History).* Rosen Publishing Group, 2003.

King, David C. *First People.* DK Children, 2008.

Kissock, Heather. *Comanche (American Indian Art and Culture).* Weigl Publishers Inc., 2010.

Lacey, Theresa Jensen. *The Comanche (The History & Culture of Native Americans).* Chelsea House Publishers, 2010.

Murdoch, David S. *North American Indian (DK Eyewitness Books).* DK Children, 2005.

Schach, David. *Comanche Warriors (History's Greatest Warriors).* Bellwether Media, 2011.

THINGS TO THINK ABOUT AND DO

EYEWITNESS TO HISTORY

Pretend you are a U.S. Army scout in 1835 on the Great Plains. You are on a hilltop waiting while a big buffalo herd of hundreds of thousands of animals is passing by. Write a short letter home telling your relatives what you are seeing.

YOU ARE THERE

Pretend you are a newspaper reporter in 1870 with a group of American buffalo hunters. Write a short news story about what they are doing and what impact that is having on the Comanche way of life.

FARAWAY FRIENDS

Pretend you are a farm boy or girl in Pennsylvania in 1890. The Indian boarding school nearby has given your father a Comanche boy to work on the family farm for the summer. He doesn't know very much English, isn't used to American food, is very homesick for his relatives, and sleeps in your father's barn with your pony. Write a short fiction story about working with him that summer.

DESIGN A PARFLECHE

Look at the picture of the Comanche parfleche on page 25. Using a colorful pattern, design your own parfleche.

INDEX

47